HOME RUN

The Science Behind Baseball's Most Amazing Plays

by Eric Braun

CAPSTONE PRESS
a capstone imprint

Published by Capstone Press, an imprint of Capstone
1710 Roe Crest Drive, North Mankato, Minnesota 56003
capstonepub.com

Copyright © 2025 by Capstone. All rights reserved. No part of this publication may be reproduced in whole or in part, or stored in a retrieval system, or transmitted in any form or by any means, electronic, mechanical, photocopying, recording, or otherwise, without written permission of the publisher.

SPORTS ILLUSTRATED KIDS is a trademark of ABG-SI LLC. Used with permission.

Library of Congress Cataloging-in-Publication Data
Names: Braun, Eric, author. Title: Home run : the science behind baseball's most amazing plays / by Eric Braun.
Description: North Mankato, Minnesota : Capstone Press, [2025]
Series: Sports illustrated kids. Science behind the plays | Includes bibliographical references and index.
Audience: Ages 8-11 | Audience: Grades 4-6
Summary: "Derek Jeter's brilliant toss to the catcher to prevent a score. Ozzie Smith's bare-handed stop and throw to first base for a critical out. Nomar Mazara's home run that sailed 505 feet. Willie Mays's legendary catch in center field. Behind every pitch, swing, catch, throw, and slide, science is at work. Dive into each of these iconic baseball plays and learn more about energy, forces, motion, and more"—Provided by publisher.
Identifiers: LCCN 2024020619 (print) LCCN 2024020620 (ebook) ISBN 9781669091936 (hardcover) | ISBN 9781669092018 (paperback) ISBN 9781669091974 (pdf) | ISBN 9781669092032 (kindle edition) ISBN 9781669092025 (epub)
Subjects: LCSH: Baseball—History—Juvenile literature. | Sports sciences—Juvenile literature. Classification: LCC GV867.5 .B728 2025 (print)
LCC GV867.5 (ebook) |DDC 796.357—dc23/eng/20240515
LC record available at https://lccn.loc.gov/2024020619
LC ebook record available at https://lccn.loc.gov/2024020620

Editorial Credits
Editor: Christianne Jones; Designer: Jaime Willems; Media Researchers: Morgan Walters and Svetlana Zhurkin; Production Specialist: Whitney Schaefer

Image Credits
Associated Press: 26, 27, File/Eric Risberg, cover (left), 8, Jeffrey McWhorter, cover (right), 21, 23, Winslow Townson, 11; Getty Images: Allsport/Al Bello, 1, 7, Bettmann, 28, 29, Dmytro Aksonov, 5, Focus on Sport, 13, GeorgiosArt, 9 (Newton), MLB Photos/Dan Donovan, 17, MLB Photos/Rich Pilling, 16, Ron Jenkins, 22, Transcendental Graphics/Mark Rucker, 19, Tribune News Service/Fort Worth Star-Telegram/Stefan Stevenson, 20; Library of Congress: 18; Shutterstock: 104000, 14, BullpenAl, cover (sand), Designua, 15, Deviney Designs (powder), cover and throughout, lumyai l sweet, 9 (referee), Marina Sun (math background), cover and throughout, noraismail, 25, Vlad Klok (baseball), back cover and throughout

Any additional websites and resources referenced in this book are not maintained, authorized, or sponsored by Capstone. All product and company names are trademarks™ or registered® trademarks of their respective holders.

Printed and bound in the USA. PO 6121

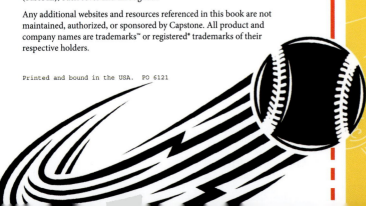

TABLE OF CONTENTS

Science and Baseball..................................... 4

Chapter One
The Flip 6

Chapter Two
A Bare-Handed Stop 12

Chapter Three
505 Feet.. 18

Chapter Four
The Catch 24

Glossary.. 30
Read More 31
Internet Sites 31
Index... 32
About the Author.................................... 32

Words in **BOLD** are in the glossary.

SCIENCE AND BASEBALL

The crack of the bat. The thrill of an amazing catch. The power of a monster home run. These are some of the most well-loved sounds and sights of baseball.

But there's more to an iconic baseball play than meets the eye. The superstar player gets all the credit. But behind every pitch, swing, catch, and throw, science is at work. **Energy**, **force**, and **motion** are key elements to every play on the field.

Let's explore how science affected some of the most memorable plays in baseball history.

DEFINITIONS

motion: the act of moving or having momentum

force: an action that changes or maintains the motion of a body or object

energy: force that causes things to move

CHAPTER ONE

THE FLIP

It was the seventh inning of Game 3 of the 2001 American League (AL) Division Series. The New York Yankees were down two games to none against the Oakland A's. And then, Oakland outfielder Terrence Long hit a hard drive into the right field corner. Oakland base runner Jeremy Giambi took off from first base. He was set on scoring.

As Giambi raced toward third base, Yankees shortstop Derek Jeter ran toward the first base line. It looked like he was moving out of position. The right fielder's throw came in a bit wild. The first baseman couldn't reach it. It looked like Giambi would score, but that's not what happened.

Jeter ran toward the overthrow. He nabbed the ball on a bounce. Then in one fluid motion, he turned and flipped it toward home plate. It was a perfect **redirection** of the path of the ball.

Terrence Long used energy, force, and motion to send the ball deep into right field.

DEFINITIONS

redirection: to change the course or direction of something using energy and motion

Posada (right) applies the tag to Giambi's leg as Jeter looks on.

Yankee's catcher Jorge Posada grabbed the flip just before Giambi crossed the plate. Catch. Swipe. Tag. The runner was out! It seemed like a magical play. But it wasn't magic. It was Jeter's instinct for being in the right place. It was also science. In fact, it involved Newton's first law of science.

In the flip play, the Yankees' right fielder applied force to the ball when he fired his throw to the infield. That was Shane Spencer. His legs, torso, and arms worked together to create that force. As the ball flew, another force affected it. That force was **gravity**. Gravity is a force that pulls objects toward the ground.

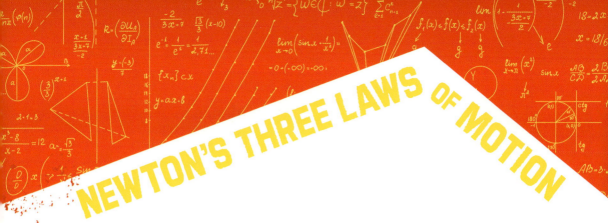

NEWTON'S THREE LAWS OF MOTION

Scientist Isaac Newton developed three rules about motion. These are known as Newton's laws of motion, and they play a huge role in every game.

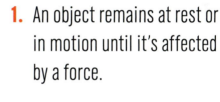

1. An object remains at rest or in motion until it's affected by a force.

2. The greater the mass of an object, the more force it will take to move it. In other words, force equals mass times acceleration ($F = ma$).

3. For every action, there is an equal and opposite reaction.

An object's motion provides **evidence** to **predict** its future motion. Seeing the throw, Jeter made a prediction that the ball would fly over the first baseman's head. If that happened, the runner would likely score.

So Jeter made sure he was in place to change the motion of the ball. He caught it, briefly applying a new force to it. It was an opposite force that stopped the ball in his glove. The energy of the ball was **transferred** to his glove. When Jeter flipped the ball toward home plate, he used his arm to apply another force to the ball. That force turned out to be the perfect touch.

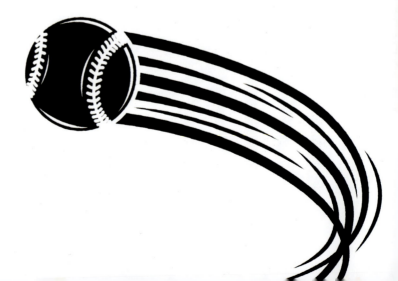

Infielders like Derek Jeter must use the perfect amount of force when making short throws or flips to their teammates.

FACT

Had Giambi scored, the A's would have been in great position to win the game and the entire series. Instead, the Yankees went on to win that game and the series.

CHAPTER TWO

A BARE-HANDED STOP

Derek Jeter used the evidence of the ball's motion to predict its future motion. But what happens when the ball's path is interrupted by a different force? Let's dig into this scenario with the help of shortstop Ozzie Smith.

On April 20, 1978, Smith was only 10 games into his career. He was playing shortstop for the San Diego Padres. Atlanta hitter Jeff Burroughs stepped up to the plate and smoked a ball up the middle. Based on its motion, its future direction was easy to predict. A sure-fire single to center field, right? Wrong!

A line drive between second and third base was no match for shortstop Ozzie Smith.

Smith darted to his left and dove for the ball. Just as he did, the ball hit a rock. Newton's third law of motion states that for every action, there is an equal and opposite reaction.

Until that moment, the rock was affected by two forces. Gravity was pulling it down, and the ground was pushing it up. It was not moving. But every object has **potential energy**.

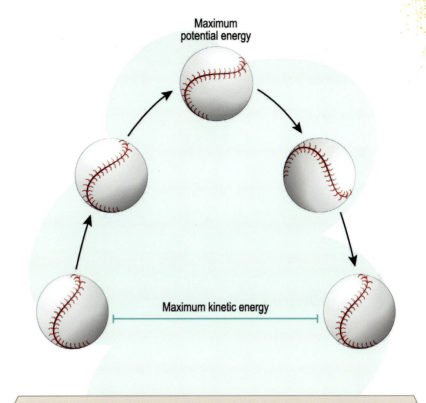

When the ball hit the rock, an equal and opposite amount of the rock's energy went into the ball. That turned the rock's potential energy into **kinetic energy**. The rock's motion caused the ball to move in a different direction.

potential energy: stored energy

kinetic energy: the energy of motion

Energy and force helped Smith launch the ball toward first base.

By the time the ball hit the rock, Smith was already in motion. His glove was ready to catch the ball where it should have gone. But the ball changed direction. Smith had no play except to reach out with his bare hand.

In a split second, Smith grabbed the ball. His hand applied its own equal and opposite force to stop the ball in flight long enough for him to trap it with his fingers. He got up quickly and fired the ball to first base. The runner was out!

FACT

Ozzie Smith was known as "the Wizard." He combined his athletic ability with acrobatic skill, making him one of the greatest shortstops of all time.

CHAPTER THREE

505 FEET

Amazing defensive plays can be poetry in motion. But sometimes you just want to see a ball explode off the bat. Home runs are the purest form of power in baseball. So who hit the longest home run in history? There are a few ways to answer that question.

On April 4, 1919, Babe Ruth of the New York Yankees hit an historic home run against the New York Giants.

The longest shot on record was hit by Babe Ruth in 1919. That rocket traveled a reported 575 feet. But that measurement is just an estimate, as there wasn't good technology for measuring hits at that time.

FACT

Statistics from the Negro Leagues were not recognized by MLB until 2020. If we include the Negro Leagues, catcher Josh Gibson would have the longest home run. He reportedly hit a 580-foot home run in 1937.

How about the longest home run since the beginning of the Statcast era? That was hit by Nomar Mazara of the Texas Rangers. It happened on June 21, 2019, during the first inning of a game against the Chicago White Sox.

THE STATCAST SYSTEM

Statcast technology came to all 30 MLB stadiums in 2015. It's a system of cameras and radar. This system allows MLB to track and put a number to most things that happen on the field. It can tell you how fast a ball was hit and how fast a runner ran. It can tell you how fast a ball was spinning and how much a curveball curved. It can tell you how quickly a catcher got off his throw to second base and how that compares to other catchers in the game.

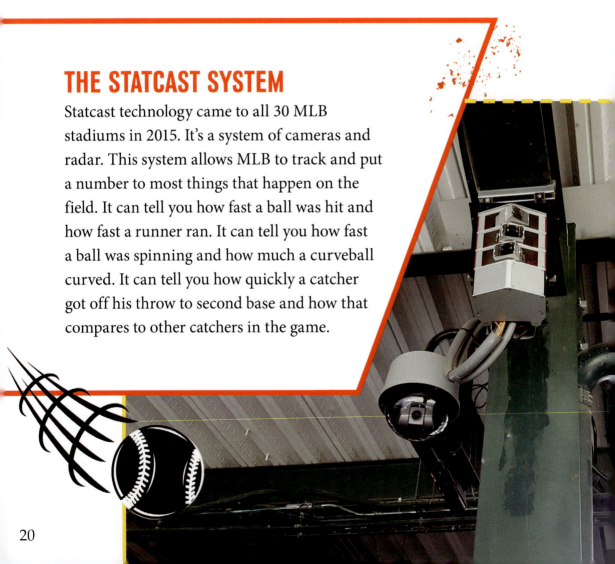

López's pitches are powered by motion from his entire body that is transferred to the ball.

Pitcher Reynaldo López fired a 95-mile-per-hour fastball toward the plate. Mazara knocked that ball 505 feet. That's about the length of two city blocks. As usual, science was at work behind the scenes.

When López threw that fastball, he applied major force on the ball. He started by reaching back with the ball in his hand. Then he stepped forward. His arm traveled forward with the ball. All of this was his way of creating a force that pushed the ball forward. The ball in motion contained a lot of energy from that force.

Mazara's strong swing sent force to the bat, which changed to energy.

When Mazara swung, he created his own force on the bat. That force put a lot of energy into the bat. When the ball and bat **collided**, there was a big transfer of energy. Some of the energy turned into sound. That's the crack of the bat you hear. The harder the hit, the louder the sound will be. That's because there's more energy being transferred.

collide: to hit with force when moving

But only some of the energy goes into the sound. The rest goes into the ball, sending it in the opposite direction. As the ball flew, gravity was a force pulling it down. The air itself also applied a force, pushing against the ball as it flew. That force slowed the ball down. Still, Mazara's ball flew at about 110 miles per hour. It landed in the very back of the upper deck.

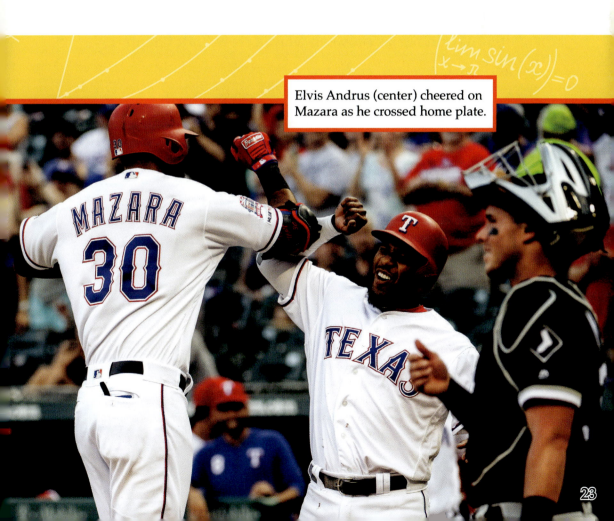

Elvis Andrus (center) cheered on Mazara as he crossed home plate.

CHAPTER FOUR

THE CATCH

In the history of baseball, there is only one play known by the simple nickname "The Catch." This play was made by Willie Mays during Game 1 of the 1954 World Series between Mays's New York Giants and the Cleveland Indians.

The score was tied 2–2 in the eighth inning. Runners were on first and second. Cleveland slugger Vic Wertz crushed a fly ball to deep center field. The force he made by swinging the bat charged the ball with energy, causing it to fly far and fast.

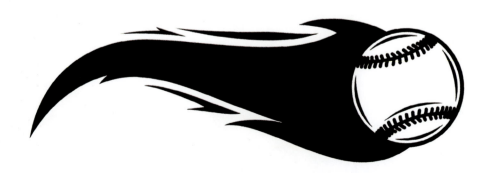

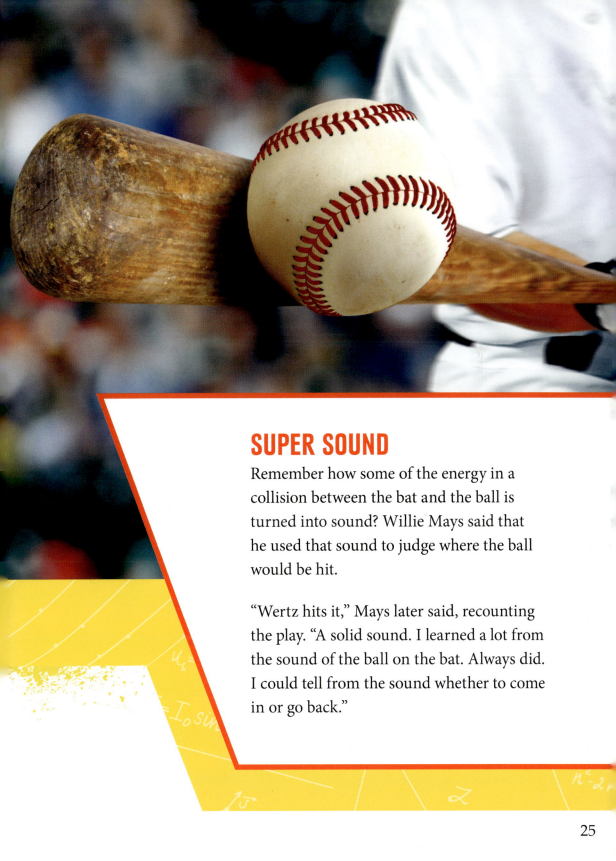

SUPER SOUND

Remember how some of the energy in a collision between the bat and the ball is turned into sound? Willie Mays said that he used that sound to judge where the ball would be hit.

"Wertz hits it," Mays later said, recounting the play. "A solid sound. I learned a lot from the sound of the ball on the bat. Always did. I could tell from the sound whether to come in or go back."

Mays had been playing a shallow center field. He was ready to quickly scoop up anything in front of him and prevent the runners from scoring. When Wertz hit that ball, Mays turned and ran toward the center field wall at full speed.

Mays sprinted, his back to the infield. The only forces acting to slow down the ball were applied by gravity, pulling it slowly down, and the air. Even though air feels like nothing, it is made of **molecules**. Those molecules are "objects" that apply their own equal and opposite force on anything that moves through them, including a high-flying baseball.

molecule: the smallest unit of substance containing one or more atoms

Mays used his experience to judge how gravity and air were slowly changing the direction of the ball. Still on the run, he put out his glove. Plop. The ball landed softly in it. And Mays wasn't done. He still had to get the ball back to the infield to prevent the runner on second base from scoring.

Mays had been sprinting at full speed. To stop quickly, he had to apply an incredible amount of force on his body in the opposite direction of which he'd been moving. He changed his long strides to short steps. Each step pushed back against his **momentum**. It took only three quick steps to stop enough so he could turn and fire a perfect throw to second base.

momentum: the force or speed created by movement

Mays's throw cut through the air, fighting gravity to reach the infield quickly. It arrived on target and in time to prevent anyone from scoring. The Giants won the game in the bottom of the tenth inning and swept the series in four games.

Baseball is a sport that never stops surprising fans with moments of beauty and grace. Pitches flying faster than a freight train. Hits rocketing off the bat. Amazing catches and throws. Science lies beneath it all, helping us understand just how that beauty and grace is created.

GLOSSARY

collide (kuh-LYED)—to hit with force when moving

energy (EH-nuhr-jee)—force that causes things to move

evidence (EH-vuh-duhns)—information, items, and facts that help prove something to be true or false

force (FOHRS)—an action that changes or maintains the motion of a body or object

gravity (GRAH-vuh-tee)—an invisible force that pulls objects toward each other; Earth's gravity pulls objects toward the ground

kinetic energy (ki-NET-ik EH-nuhr-jee)—the energy of motion

molecule (MAH-luh-kyool)—the smallest unit of a substance, containing one or more atoms

momentum (moh-MEN-tuhm)— the force or speed created by movement

motion (MOH-shuhn)—the act of moving or having momentum

potential energy (puh-TEN-shuhl EH-nuhr-jee)— stored energy

predict (prih-DIKT)—to figure out in advance what will happen

redirection (ree-dih-REK-shuhn)—to change the course or direction of something using energy and motion

transfer (TRANS-fuhr)—to move from one object to another

READ MORE

Berglund, Bruce. *Baseball GOATs: The Greatest Athletes of All Time.* North Mankato, MN: Capstone, 2022.

Helget, N. *Full STEAM Baseball: Science, Technology, Engineering, Arts, and Mathematics of the Game.* North Mankato, MN: Capstone, 2019.

Van, R. L. *Baseball Then and Now.* Minneapolis: Abdo Publishing, 2024.

INTERNET SITES

Exploratorium: Science of Baseball
annex.exploratorium.edu/baseball

Major League Baseball
mlb.com

National Baseball Hall of Fame
baseballhall.org

INDEX

energy, 4, 14–16
evidence, 10, 12

force, 4, 7–9, 10–12,
    16, 21–24, 26, 28

Giambi, Jeremy, 6, 8, 11
Gibson, Josh, 19
gravity, 8, 23, 26–27, 29

Jeter, Derek, 6–8, 10–12

kinetic energy, 15

Long, Terrence, 6–7
López, Reynaldo, 21

Mays, Willie, 24–27
Mazara, Nomar, 20–23
molecules, 26
momentum, 4, 28
motion, 4, 7, 9, 10, 12,
    14–16, 18, 21, 29

Negro Leagues, 19
Newton's laws of motion,
    8–9, 14, 29

Posada, Jorge, 8
potential energy, 14–15
predict, 10, 12

reaction, 9, 14
redirection, 7
Ruth, Babe, 18–19

Smith, Ozzie, 12–14, 16–17
speed, 26, 28
Spencer, Shane, 8
Statcast era, 20

technology, 19–20
transfer, 10, 21–22

Wertz, Vic, 24–25

ABOUT THE AUTHOR

Eric Braun is a children's author and editor. He has written dozens of books on many topics, and one of his books was read by an astronaut on the International Space Station for kids on Earth to watch. Eric lives in Minneapolis with his wife, two kids, and a dog that is afraid of cardboard.